The Ultimate Guide to Digital Marketing

A Business Owners Guide to online marketing

Joe Burns

FIRST EDITION

Contents

Introduction

How do you find more customers for your business?

Your business doesn't just grow on its own, well you probably know that by now anyway. Sure, you'll receive small incremental amounts of growth through word of mouth but if you really want to start growing your business in a way that's both fast and long lasting, you'll want to stick around.

Not everyone will be able to make a video which goes viral and immediately receive 100,000 new likes on their Facebook page. Even a £100,000 marketing budget isn't going to be much use if you spend it 'trying' 1000 new tactics.

I'm sure you've seen these expensive courses advertised online, some charging £5,000 for a bunch of videos claiming to teach you everything you could ever need to know about Digital Marketing. Believe me - They're a waste of money.

Rest assured, by the end of this book, whether you're a computer whiz or know next to nothing when it comes to IT, you'll be able to confidently run your businesses digital marketing.

Who Am I?

I'm Joe, I grew up in Essex and have always had a passion for IT.

When I was just 15, I decided to dive into the realm of Digital Marketing, more specifically web design. At the time I was building and managing a website for a family member. Quickly there became a need for me to learn online marketing techniques to be able to promote this website and gain more customers for their business.

I then spent the next few years developing my Digital Marketing skills. During this time, I gained experience marketing for several different businesses across a range of industries.

I have written this book with the aim of helping business owners and marketers across all industries to be able to grow their business online without the need to pay an agency or somebody else lots of money to do it for them. Sure, there will be aspects which will be challenging, but I am going to show you how to do everything right here.

What is Digital Marketing?

If I asked you to think about the amount of people that use the internet today, I'm sure you would come up with an extremely high number, but would you believe me if I told you that the number people that go online every day is still increasing?

Well, for every day in the past five years, an average of 640,000 people accessed the internet for the first time. That's 233,600,000 new people using the internet every year!

The internet has changed the way people shop, whether it's buying an e-book from Amazon, purchasing an item on eBay or even ordering your Friday night takeaway by using an app on your phone. This all means that offline marketing is no longer as effective as it used to be.

For example, say you own an equestrian riding school aimed at young children. You pay a radio station to play your advert it may reach 10,000 people. Of those 10,000 people maybe only 5,000 may have young children. Of those 5,000 maybe only 1,000 have a child who is interested in riding lessons, and of that 1,000 maybe only 600 parents can afford the riding lessons.

You can see how although you've been able to get your message across to lots of people, only a very small percentage of that group are actually interested in your product/service.

What if there was a way to instead target 10,000 people who have already shown an interest in your industry, or a particular product/service you sell? You would much rather get your message across to that audience, wouldn't you?

Meet Digital Marketing

Digital Marketing is a broad term used to describe all aspects of marketing online, I have listed some below that we are going to cover in this book.

- Website Design
- Search Engine Optimisation (SEO)
- Search Engine Advertising (SEA)

- Social Media Marketing (SMM)
- Pay Per Click (PPC)
- Email Marketing
- Lead Generation Marketing (LGM)
- Content Marketing

Sure, you could use just one of these methods, but that wouldn't provide you with the best results. It's when you combine all of these marketing strategies that you really begin to leverage what's possible in this new digital age.

Digital Marketing can work for any business, in any industry. To run a successful business, you need to always stay ahead of your competition, give yourself an edge. It is vital that you stay ahead of the times, no matter what kind of business you run.

Gone are the days that only large corporate companies with huge marketing budgets were able to advertise online. Digital marketing gives small to medium size businesses a fighting chance to compete with them by targeting a specific niche and finding the people who are most likely to turn into customers for you.

Digital Marketing is vital for your business and brand awareness. If you look at all your competitors, I'd be extremely confident that most if not all of them already have a website, if they don't, they will at least have a social media presence or a digital advertising strategy. Online content for businesses is no longer just a marketing tool, it's something that customers expect to see and quite often rely on. Whether it's to get information regarding opening hours, comparing menus on where to eat tonight or maybe trying to find reviews for your business, you can be sure they'll be doing it online.

By using Digital Marketing you're also able to view analytics on how well your marketing is going. You're able to use the many tools which I will show you to ultimately calculate precise ROI's (Return on Investments) so that you know which strategies are proving effective, and which ones aren't.

Where to start? – The Importance of a Website.

Your website is the central place that you want to be sending your traffic from all your different social outlets, like Facebook and Twitter.

Think of your website as your digital shopfront. When somebody wants to find a piece of information they are more often or not turning to the internet to find it. When somebody searches for something that you offer, or even specifically your business, you want to show up. Not only show up but show up looking good.

Your website is often the first impression of your business that your potential customer will get. For traffic coming from Google, or a link they've found, your website will be the first point of contact they have with your business. People form an opinion very quickly about you and your business based on the information they first see. For example, if a customer walks past your physical store and sees it run down, dirty and not looked after but there is another store right across the street which has recently been refurbished they are probably going to go to that one. It's the same with the internet, except there isn't just one store across the street, there are thousands of them.

There are a couple of key principles you need to keep in mind when creating a website or evaluating the one you currently have. Your website must be:

- Clean
- Well-Organised
- Easy to navigate
- Concise and to the point
- Modern
- Functional
- Branded
- Linked well to your other platforms (Social Media Accounts, any Apps associated with your business)

The user viewing your website wants to find a quick solution to their problem or an answer to their question. You need to remember that your business is based upon solving a problem of the customer. For example, if you are running a MOT Garage, your customer's problem is the fact that they need a MOT. You need to make it as quick and as easy as possible for them to solve that problem. If your website is too complicated and cluttered, they are likely to leave and go to another website.

Studies have shown that once a user clicks onto a website, they will either click off within 10 seconds, or spend a considerable amount of time browsing and eventually buying your service/product. There's little in-between. Why do you think this is?

This is because with so much information available to individuals on the internet, they do not have the patience to be trawling through a cluttered disorganised website. They take one look at the home page and decide whether they will be able to find a solution to their problem quickly. Make it easy for them. There is a saying which I very much agree with – Those that are confused do not buy.

If there's a question that you are asked over and over again by potential clients put it on the home page as a big bold header. Attract your users' attention to it, it's probably a question that they have too! Once they've read the answer to that question, they are more likely to keep reading through your website as they've already invested their time with you.

People also want to look at something that's visually appealing and easy to read. Limit the fancy fonts that *might look good.* Do not compromise usability for aesthetics. A good quality website should look good whether you're viewing it on a phone, tablet or computer as well as different browsers (Safari, Google Chrome, Firefox etc). Make sure to test your website on all the devices and browsers your potential customers might be using as you want to keep as many customers on your website for as long as you can. The longer they are there the more likely they are to buy from you.

A good website is well polished. There should be no spelling or grammatical errors. No childish clip art, blurry pictures or design traits that look like they're from the 80's (Best to cancel the plans for a luminous green font on a red background with flashing clipart behind it!). Before you allow your website to be visible to the public your content must be complete and must be visually appealing.

It is important to invest enough time and money into your website when you are creating it as it will be a lasting asset that won't age very quickly. Especially with regular content updates and website management, you can expect to be able to use your same website for at least 15 years – maybe even longer!

With 93% of all purchase decisions starting with a search engine search, the ease of access for your potential customers to find information relevant to your business and the low cost per impression on your website there is really no way your business can live without one.

So where can you get one?

There are realistically two options available to you (unless you're a programming mastermind!). Either hire a professional Web Designer/Agency or turn to an online website builder to do it yourself. I'll explain the advantages and disadvantages of both.

When you use a Web Designer/Agency you can almost guarantee that the finished product will be a professional, clean and well-functioning website. A good web design team will first have a deep dive discovery session with you to determine your goals and learn the ins and outs of your business. They should then formulate a personalised strategy for exactly how they will design and build your website to match your goals.

Using a Web Designer/Agency will allow you an unlimited amount of customisation as well as access to more complex features that you won't be able to get anywhere else, like complicated back end management systems. Your agency will be able to optimise your website with say what the words are then put the acronym in brackets (SEO) in mind right from the start so that you're in the best position when you launch your website.

Unfortunately, a custom website from a Web Design Agency is no small cost. In the UK you can expect to pay between £2,000 - £15,000 for a good quality website. That may seem a lot but when you think about the price an average physical shop front would set you back, plus the fact that this digital shopfront has the potential to be shown to millions more potential customers, it suddenly doesn't seem that expensive.

After hearing the cost of a bespoke website, you may be thinking that an online service such as 'WIX' might be your best bet, and maybe it is. Online website builders allow you to create a website with little IT knowledge, it's as simple as creating a PowerPoint presentation. You just drag and drop text boxes, images and whatever you want on your website. The draw back comes with customisability. You can easily tell when a website is from an online builder – they all look the same. You must follow a template set out by the website builder with no room to put in your own designs.

When it comes to marketing, using a website built by an online website builder means that your options become limited very quickly. There is little scope to build an email subscription, and performing effective SEO is practically impossible. Though online web builders will try to get you to buy an SEO package, this will do nowhere near as much for your business as a proper agency developing a custom SEO strategy.

Usually with these sites there will be a monthly cost that you'll have to pay for your website instead of an upfront cost. You'll then have to keep these payments up as long as you want the website to be live.

Do take caution though; Once you've built a website in an online builder it is very difficult to migrate that website to another platform. They want you to stay with them. I know, cheeky right?

Getting people to see your website – Search Engine Optimisation (SEO)

SEO in basic terms means getting quality traffic onto your website through the use of ranking organically I don't know what this means. Will the reader? in searches on major search engines like Google. You see this implemented every time you make a search. For example, say you search for Plumbers in London, you are probably only going to look at the top three or so results. Maybe even just the top one! This is why it is so important for you to be ranking at the top for the searches that your potential customers are making!

Google or the search engine that you are using has something called a web spider. This spider crawls through websites on the internet gathering lots of information about the websites it's on. It'll gather data on how quickly the site loads, how many times a specific keyword is mentioned, whether your sentences make sense and millions of other bits of information. The crawler then reports all that information back to the search engine to build up an index. An algorithm will then try to match your search to the most appropriate website.

If you search for 'Homemade Vegan Chocolate Middlesbrough', Google is more likely to display a website that uses that phrase 20 times than one that only mentions it once. I'm sure you are now beginning to understand how this all works.

In simple terms, the algorithms of the search engines are trying to determine what the most relevant website is to display for any given search.

The first thing to understand in order to rank your website higher on search engines is that Google and others rank pages, not websites. Just because your business makes wooden counter tops doesn't mean that every page on your site should rank for 'Wooden Counter Tops'.

When performing SEO on your website the first thing you need to do is improve the website's crawlability. Before a search engine can rank your site it needs to actually know it exists. There are several ways that search engines discover sites, one of which we have already mentioned, crawling. The spiders will prioritise links on pages that the search engine already knows over one that they haven't crawled before.

For example, your homepage has a backlink (a link from another website to your website) on a website that has already been crawled by Google. Next time Google crawls that site they will come across your site and you'll be added to Google's index.

From there they'll follow the internal links on your site in order to crawl your whole website. You want as much of your website crawled as often as possible so it's essential that you make sure every page of your website is linked together properly.

Luckily for you there is an easy way for you to check your site's crawlability. I have listed the steps below.

1. Visit https://search.google.com/search-console/about
2. Sign up and verify your website
3. Navigate to where it says 'Coverage'

4. Any errors will be displayed in the red error box along with a guide on how to fix them.

63% of all Search Engine Searches come through a mobile device. Search Engines evaluate how mobile friendly your website is. So, make sure that your website looks good and functions well on a mobile device.

When checking whether a website looks good on a mobile, I find that using an online emulator works best. It allows you to view your website from a range of different devices. Both Safari and Google have this feature built in. Just go to 'Develop" and select 'Responsive Design Mode'. From there you're able to use the drop-down menu to choose which device you would like to view the website from.

The speed of which your website loads is another major factor when it comes to ranking your page. Nobody wants to be waiting 3 minutes for your website to load, and Search Engines know that too!

You can check your page speed by following the steps below:

1. Visit https://search.google.com/search-console/about
2. Login
3. Navigate to Page Speed Insights
4. An orange pie chart will pop up showing you how fast your website loads.

If your web page is showing as loading 'too slow' it's nothing to worry about, it can be sorted in a few easy steps. First make sure you have cache enabled. Depending on which route you took getting your website either look for an option on your website building dashboard or ask your Web Design Agency if they are enabled.

Cache allows browsers to save data from your website to individual websites allowing for faster loading times when a user visits that website again.

You can also look at your images, if you're using high resolution images there's nothing wrong with using a compression tool to lower the size of them. The smaller the file size, the quicker your load times will be. You can find a compression tool just by searching 'Image Compression Tool' on Google.

If your website is loading slowly you may also want to consider your web hosting package. Reach out to your hosting provider and tell them the situation. They may offer a better package for free or give you some useful tips to get the most out of your existing package.

One of the most vital steps to take when performing SEO on your website is keyword research and planning.

You need to consider what phrases your potential customers are typing into Search Engines. It's a good idea to put yourself in your customer's shoes. If you were in their position, with their problem, what would you search. Open a word document and write all of these phrases down. Try and get as specific as you can. For example, if one of your phrases is 'Child Minder Dorset' get even more specific and use town names.

The reason I suggest doing this is because it's easier to rank for keyword with lower competition. Don't get me wrong, I'm not saying that you shouldn't rank for the highest competition keywords but ranking for lower competition keywords begins to build your credibility with Search Engines.

Search Engines will look at where you rank for other search queries as well as how much traffic you are getting onto your website. By ranking for lower competition keywords, you are building up the amount of traffic you are receiving. The beauty is that once you rank for a phrase, the traffic will compound and keep coming month after month.

So now you've got a list of phrases, it's time to implement them.

Look through your list and find the most specific phrase you have written. You are able to check how competitive a phrase is by using 'Google Keyword Planner'. It's a very simple application, you just type in the phrase and it shows you a list of phrases associated with your search along with the number of monthly searches and the level of competition.

The lowest competition phrase is the one that you want rank for first. Begin by reading through your website and find places where you mention that phrase and where you mention relevant topics.

Add the phrase you are trying to rank for in the headings of all relevant paragraphs. This tells Search Engines that there's relevant content here and so they should display that content. Be careful about overusing your phrase in headings as Search Engine Algorithms are good at spotting a phrase that's just been crammed in repeatedly. Make sure that you're only adding that phrase to relevant headers and ensure that they always make sense otherwise you may be penalised in search and find it harder to rank higher.

Now that you have your headers optimised you should optimise your content. Taking the same steps as above you want to mention that phrase as many times as makes sense. You can also use variations of that phrase, they will still count towards your rank.

One of the great SEO tools is a having a blog on your website that you regularly update. If you have one, try to write as many articles as you can containing your phrase. This helps with your relevance to Search Engines as you're showing that you have lots of information relevant to what your potential customers are searching for. Here's a couple of tips for writing SEO friendly blog articles.

1. Structure your blog post into different clearly defined sections
2. Carefully design your Title and Meta Description – It's most likely the first thing your readers will see.
3. Use headings appropriately
4. Keep paragraphs short and concise
5. Be sure to link to sources and other websites where appropriate
6. Link to other pages of your own website! This gets the spiders to crawl through more of your content which is very important.
7. Make use of your keywords but avoid keyword cramming
8. Longer blog articles perform better so try to go in-depth when writing your article

The title the page on your website is displayed on search engines. It should accurately describe what is on the page so that the user is able to know exactly what to expect if they click on your website. Keep your title between 40-55 characters long and be sure to use proper spelling and grammar. When looking at your website from a HTML view, your title will be within a <title> tag. If you are using an Online Website Builder there should be an option within the settings window.

"MOT testing from just £30 | Example MOT's | Fully Accredited MOT Garage"

This title first has a hook, something that grabs the user's eye. In this case they are promoting a good offer which entices the user to read further. The rest of the title is very clear and short. Their company name and a short sentence about why you should trust them – to build credibility in the user's mind. Notice that the word "MOT" has been used three times? This is how you should be using your keywords.

Along with the title, every page should have a meta description. This is the short paragraph below the link to your website displayed on Search Engines. It has been shown that websites with a meta description perform up to 90% better than those without.

Your meta description is within a <meta> tag when being viewed from html. Similarly, you may be able to access this option from the settings window on an Online Website builder.

When writing a meta description keep your paragraph clear and concise. Try to summarise what the purpose of your website is in as few words as possible. A good way to write a description is to think about what your customer's problems are, like the MOT garage example:

> *"Looking for a local garage you can trust? Book an appointment today with Example MOT Garage today! – A trusted, Fully accredited, RAC approved MOT garage."*

This description is clear. You know exactly what to expect upon clicking a link to that website. There is a call to action asking the user directly to book an appointment, and then another sentence about why they are a trust worthy company. It's important to continually build up credibility in your potential customers' minds so that when they do eventually come to buy from you there is an element of trust already there.

So, now you have begun to build up credibility in your potential customers' minds, it's time to do the same with Search Engines. You do this by building backlinks.

Backlinks are where another website already known by the search engine links to one of your website's pages. The more sites that link to your page, the more reliable Search Engines will perceive your content to be. Backlinks are also ranked based on how credible the website that is linking to your website is. A backlink from one of the top websites in your industry is far more valuable than a backlink from a small website that nobody's heard of.

There are a couple of ways to build backlinks, the simplest of which is to just ask for one. The way to do this is by finding content on the internet which is relevant to your topic. Once you've found a relevant web page, look for where the author is credited and make a note of their name. If there is no name on the article just navigate to the 'contact' section and find an email address.

Compose an email and express your interest in their chosen subject and mention that you have some information on your website that might be useful to a reader. Then suggest that it may be beneficial for them to add a link to your website within their article. You would be surprised how many people are willing to do this.

Another way to build backlinks when you are an expert on a certain subject is to interact with online communities. Find forums dedicated to your industry and start answering people's questions. Within those questions you should link to relevant content from your own site. Some big forum websites such as Quora do not allow backlinks, they employ something called no-follow links. This means that when Google crawls that forum they will not follow the link and crawl your site. Especially when you become a credible contributor to a specific industry – you'll have people begging to link to your content.

The last step to performing Search Engine Optimisation on your website is to set up analytical tracking. This will allow you to track how many visitors you are receiving onto your website as well as the keyword they are putting into the Search Engine to find your website. This will allow you to see which of your phrases are performing well, and which ones you need to work on.

One tool that I use is Google Analytics. This tool is free to use and is very simple. Here's how to get it set up:

1. Go to https://anayltics.google.com
2. Sign up or login
3. Verify your website if prompted
4. Navigate to 'Overview'

Here you will be able to see a range of data such as how many people have visited your website, what searches they used to find you, what other sources people are using to access your website (Facebook, Twitter etc), and lots more.

Can I pay Google to get to the top? – Pay Per Click (PPC)

Pay Per Click Advertising is where you pay a search engine to display your website as an advert just before the first organically ranked search result. You may recognise them from when you've searched before.

There are different types of PPC Adverts but the main one is Paid Search Adverts, so that's what we'll focus on here. With PPC, the business that is running the advert is only charged when somebody actually clicks on the link to your website, as opposed to when you run a Facebook advert, where you're charged based on how many people viewed the advert.

Search Engines determine whose advert to show at the top of their pages by using something called an Ad Auction. This is a completely automated process used by most search engines to find the relevance and validity of the adverts that appear on their results pages.

When you set up your advert you will choose keywords that you want your advert to appear for as well as how much you're willing to pay for each click. When anyone searches for that keyword an automatic bidding process will occur between all parties wanting to rank their website at the top of the list of adverts. This will determine which adverts appear in which order from which advertiser.

As you have to pay for every click onto your website it's important to only bid on the keywords that are actually relevant to the page you're advertising for. Otherwise your return on investment will quickly become very poor.

Due to the nature of PPC, it only works when you continue to pay for that campaign, whereas the results you gain from organic SEO will be there for life. An advantage of PPC over SEO is the fact that you have laser point accuracy when it comes to targeting. You can choose specific words that you want to appear for as well as factors getting as specific as the time of day. Creating a PPC campaign takes a very short amount of time, you could easily set up a PPC campaign and leave it to run with only an hour's work, as opposed to SEO taking days upon days just to optimise one web page.

To set up a PPC campaign you first need to determine which Search Engine you would like to advertise with. I would recommend using Google as they have the most amount of traffic passing through their site per day. Once you have found a Search Engine you then need to find their tool for advertising.

With Google it's called 'Google AdWords'. You then just need to follow the on-screen instructions in order to create your advert. It's very simple. Remember to follow the same advice for your Title and Description as outlined before in Chapter 4 –

Getting People to See Your Website – Search Engine Optimisation (SEO).

If I had to recommend PPC or SEO I would choose SEO every day. I find that being able to consistently rank your pages highly in Searches will help so much more in the process of building your web traffic.

How to launch your first successful Campaign – Social Media Marketing (SMM)

Social Media Marketing is the use of Online Social Media Outlets to connect with your potential customers, build your brand, increase the traffic to your website and ultimately result in more sales. There are hundreds of different Social Media Platforms, but when you are in the early stages of building your online presence it is only necessary to focus on the major ones: Facebook, Twitter, Instagram, Snapchat, Pinterest and YouTube.

Each of these Social Media Platforms offers unique features providing different user experiences. For example, Snapchat is designed for short (10 Second) videos or pictures that disappear after 24 Hours. Instagram allows users to post pictures or short (1 Minute) videos that stay on your profile indefinitely (Unless you delete them). It is important to understand the different features each platform provides before creating your campaigns and adverts so that you are able to create the right content for the correct audience. A great way to learn to understand a platform is to create an account and try it for yourself! If you immerse yourself in the platforms you want to advertise on, then you'll be much better equipped when it comes to creating content.

If you were running a newspaper advertising campaign you would not be expected to advertise in all of the top newspapers, but this is not the case with Digital Marketing. Your clients expect to see your business on their favourite Social Media Platforms, it can even damage your credibility if they can't find you! This is why it is so important to build a strong, diverse online presence.

The first businesses that took to Social Media used it as a broadcasting outlet, a place for them to publish content with the hope of the reader deciding to go onto buy from them, but Social Media has evolved into something much more now. You are able to engage with our potential clients speaking to them directly, listen to their views and adapt accordingly. In a business sense, Social Media can be used in a range of different ways, from market research to building brand recognition.

In this Chapter I am going to focus on Facebook. Facebook is the largest Social Media Platform with 1.69 Billion users. That's a lot of people that you have the potential to reach. It doesn't cost anything to set up a business Facebook page, and once you've created the page, you're also able to post content, link to your website and engage with your audience completely for free. This makes Facebook a great tool for any business, no matter how tight the budget is.

It is extremely easy to set up your business Facebook page, here's a step by step guide to show you how:

1. Go to www.facebook.com/pages/create
2. Choose your brand type – For most applications you will want to choose 'Local Business'
3. Enter the details of your business (Location, Contact Details etc.)
4. Add a Profile Picture and Cover Photo.
5. Complete your page description,
6. Create your username – It's best to just set it as @'YourBusiness'
7. Add a Call to Action Button

8. Publish your page

When selecting the location for your business it is paramount that you use your real address as this will be used for billing and for correspondence with Facebook. If your business is serviced based Not sure what this means – can you re-word it? or you do not want people to visit a physical location, there is a box which you are able to tick which reads 'Do not show my business address on Facebook'.

Your Profile Picture and Cover Photo should be high quality relevant photos. I would recommend having your logo on a plain background for your profile picture. You have more of creative scope when it comes to the cover photo although it should be a picture relevant to your business. For example, a MOT garage may want to use a picture of the front of their workshop. I would recommend having your logo in the top right corner as well as Social Media Icons in the lower left showing what other platforms your business is active on. This will encourage users to visit your other outlets and increase their exposure to your business.

Your Page Description can be no longer than 255 characters long. You should write a short brief description about your business including the services/products that you offer. It's a good idea to use this description to build credibility, phrases like 'Family owned business since 1940' can help with this.

A Call to Action button is critical on your Facebook Page. This is the button that appears at the top of the page right below your cover photo. You are able to customise this with many options such as: Get Quote, Contact Now, Send Message, Visit Website & More. When choosing which call to action button to use you should consider which is most relevant to your business and which method of contact you prefer. If you are a tradesman then a 'Get Quote' button may be most effective, whereas 'Visit Website' may be most suitable for an Online Shop.

 Now you have your Facebook page set up and optimised it's time to start creating content. Ideally you would be posting fresh content on your page daily but as a business owner only just starting out with Social Media this probably isn't feasible. I would suggest aiming for at least 3-5 posts per week. This allows for your page to still be classed as active while allowing you time to create quality content and focus on other business commitments.

There are several different types of posts you can publish on Facebook. There are three main posts that you should focus on: photos, videos and links. Studies have shown that people are more likely to read a post if there is a photo attached so avoid just writing statuses. Your posts should be engaging and have something that your audience can comment on. Avoid just posting about your own business and try to engage with your niche – ask your audience their thoughts on a hot topic in your niche. For example, if you are a business management consultancy, ask your audience for views on new formats for companies such as flexible working hours.

Videos have been shown over and over again to be the best converting content that you can post on Social Media. In this age people are much more inclined to watch a short video than they are to read a full article so use this to your advantage. You do not need to create a high budget production video; your phone camera should surface. Try recording yourself talking about something that your business has achieved this week, or even better something that you have helped one of your clients achieve.

Now that you have created your Facebook page it's time to exploit the number one most powerful marketing tool available today: Facebook Advertising.

This is not to be mistaken for the 'Boosting' feature you may have seen on your Facebook Page already 'for just £10 we can show this post to 10,000 more people'. Don't do it – it's not worth it. A much better place for that £10 is in Facebook Advertising which I am going to show you now.

Facebook Advertising allows you to create an advert from scratch, then choose who you want to see your advert, and then deliver your advert. You may have seen these when scrolling through Facebook before, they appear as 'Sponsored' content.

As with creating a normal post on Facebook you have a number of different options available to you. The two that you should focus on for your first campaign is Photos and Videos.

To create an effective Facebook Advertising campaign, you first want to set out a clear plan. You need to work out what your goal for this campaign is. Do you want to build brand recognition? Do you want more orders of a specific product? Or maybe you want to promote a new store location. There are hundreds of goals that you could choose.

Once you've chosen your goal you can now begin to build your advert accordingly. For this example, I have chosen the goal of 'More orders for a specific product'. The most effective advert for this will be a photo advert. I would choose a photo which clearly displays the product in its best light or maybe somebody using the product. On top of this image we would then add some text. You should take caution as Facebook does not like adverts to contain a large amount of text so keep it minimal. I would only include the price and a few words describing what the product is. You want this to stand out to the reader so that they stop scrolling and read your advert.

Once you have selected your picture you will be able to fill in other information such as the title (The bold sentence across the top) and the description. Again, the title should be engaging as to draw the reader's eye. Your description should be short and concise but clearly show the reader why they could not possibly consider passing on your offer.

Finally, I would provide a direct link to the product page on my website so that if the reader does decide that they would like to purchase this product they only need to click the link and then they can order it immediately.

Now that you have created your advert you are able to choose targeting settings based on who you want your advert to be displayed to. To target your advert efficiently you must first understand who your potential customers are. Look at the typical person who buys from your business, which age range do they fall into? What sort of occupation do they have? What area do they live in?

Once you have found out this information you are able to 'Create New Audience'. Once you have selected this option start typing your demographics into the box which reads 'Custom Audiences'. This will define the people that see your advert. You are also able to select audiences that will not see your advert. For example, if you are advertising for a Men's Shaving Cream then you may want to exclude women from the people the advert will be shown to.

By targeting your adverts, you are able to increase the efficiency of your adverts, reaching the relevant people to your business without spending money advertising to people that have no interest in any of the products/services that you offer.

How to Maintain your New-Found Online Presence?

Now that you have your Website, SEO and Social Media Marketing Campaigns set up you need to maintain them to keep them working efficiently. Nobody wants to look through a Facebook Page that hasn't been posted on since 2016, neither does anybody want to read through a website which hasn't been updated since 2000. A good way to ensure that your online presence is always maintained is to create a day by day schedule on what you need to do. For example, mark the days which you are going to post on different Social Media Platforms like Facebook and Instagram. Mark a day once a week that you'll review your website and add relevant content. Maybe you could have a day where you create all of the content for your digital campaigns for the week all at once so that they are ready to go when you need them.

It's important to keep engaged with your audience. When somebody comments on one of your pictures be sure to reply to it, even if it's negative feedback, a message apologising and making things right can go a long way. When creating new content be careful not to fall into the trap of creating repetitive posts, try to find new ways to communicate with your audience. Maybe you could host some competitions, or a daily trivia question.

As mentioned previously it's important that you continue to advance the SEO on your website, continuing to build backlinks and implementing new keywords into your website. This will ensure that your website continues to rank highly, and also improve your ranking over time for other pages.

What Next?

Some business owners simply do not have the time to manage their own Social Media Channels, and that's okay. Whether you manage it yourself or hire somebody else to do it for you, it's important to understand what they are doing so that you can see their work first hand and provide your own constructive criticism. You may now be able to point out areas that they might be neglecting and how they could improve them.

Be sure to keep in touch with me on Facebook. You can join the Facebook Group I have set up 'Digital Marketing Advice for Businesses'. This group is dedicated to UK based business owners where you are able to ask questions and others like yourself are able to share your experiences using social Media.

I wish you well with your future digital marketing journey,

Joe.